"At a superficial glance, Pier Giorgio Frassati's lifestyle, that of a modern young man who was full of life, does not present anything out of the ordinary. This, however, is the originality of his virtue, which invites us to reflect upon it and impels us to imitate it. In him faith and daily events are harmoniously fused, so that adherence to the Gospel is translated into loving care for the poor and the needy in a continual crescendo until the very last days of the sickness which led to his death. His love for beauty and art, his passion for sports and mountains, his attention to society's problems did not inhibit his constant relationship with the Absolute. Entirely immersed in the mystery of God and totally dedicated to the constant service of his neighbor: thus we can sum up his earthly life!"

> From the homily of **Pope John Paul II**, at the beatification of Pier Giorgio Frassati, May 20, 1990

"It is a rare thing to have a book that, literally, invites you to 'come outside' to read it. This refreshing invitation, drawn from the life and example of Pier Giorgio Frassati, is a field guide for anyone who chooses to embark on an adventure toward virtue. It is call to leave comfort behind and follow a beloved saint on his journey toward heaven."

> **Fr. David Michael Moses**
> Social media evangelist and guide for Hallow's
> *Saints in 7 Days with Bl. Pier Giorgio Frassati* series

"*The Frassati Field Guide* captures the essence of Pier Giorgio in an accessible and engaging read. Toss it in the backpack and head for the heights! The Church's newest saint is calling us to encounter Christ on the mountaintop."

> **Fr. John Nepil**
> Mountaineer and assistant professor at
> St. John Vianney Theological Seminary in Denver

The
Frassati
Field Guide

An 8-Day Ascent to Heroic Virtue

Bobby Angel

AVE MARIA PRESS AVE Notre Dame, Indiana

Scripture quotations are from the *Revised Standard Version of the Bible—Second Catholic Edition (Ignatius Edition)*, copyright © 2006 National Council of the Churches of Christ in the United States of America. Used by permission. All rights reserved.

Excerpts from Pier Giorgio Frassati, *Letters to His Friends and Family*, trans. Fr. Timothy E. Deeter (Alba House, 2009) used with permission of St. Paul's Publishing, 2187 Victory Blvd., Staten Island, NY 10314-6603.

All rights reserved. No part of this book may be used or reproduced in any manner whatsoever, except in the case of reprints in the context of reviews, without written permission from Ave Maria Press®, Inc., P.O. Box 428, Notre Dame, IN 46556, 1-800-282-1865.

Founded in 1865, Ave Maria Press is a ministry of the United States Province of Holy Cross.

www.avemariapress.com

Paperback: ISBN-13 978-1-64680-405-4

E-book: ISBN-13 978-1-64680-406-1

Cover image of Pier Giorgio Frassati © Wikimedia Commons.

Cover and text design by Andy Wagoner.

Printed and bound in the United States of America.

Library of Congress Cataloging-in-Publication Data is available.

For all the adventurers and
those yearning to see God:
Seek the heights!

Contents

INTRODUCTION
To the Heights!

Pier Giorgio Frassati is one of the Church's newest saints for a good reason: he was a person of bold action. There are many excellent books and resources on his life, including a few penned by his very own sister, Luciana. This field guide is not an extensive biography on Frassati, but rather an encounter with his words and actions so that we can practice the same virtues he lived. Think of this as an introduction to a new saintly friend. This resource will give you a snapshot of his life and faith and will challenge you to take action yourself. You can throw this in your backpack and head out the door to whatever adventure or wilderness (physical or spiritual) beckons at the moment.

The chapters will take you through Pier Giorgio's life: his upbringing and character, his love of the mountains, his Catholic faith and devotion to the Eucharist, his relationship with friends, family, and those on the margins (his steadfast service to the poor likely led to his contraction of the polio that killed him at the young age of twenty-four), and his enduring legacy as a saint whose witness calls us to be the hands and feet of Christ for all we meet.

This book is intended to be used in the field, so use it like Frassati would—it can handle wear and tear! When you've completed it, with St. Pier Giorgio's intercession, it will have dirt on the spine, dog-eared corners, and smudges and coffee stains on its pages. Pier Giorgio was a "man of action," and it's not enough to simply read about the life of such a disciple—let's inject the inspiration of his witness into our lives.

Structured as an eight-day retreat, this book could be read eight days in a row as part of a period of personal prayer and study, or spread out over a longer period as needed. This work will serve you best if you allow yourself time to slow down and ponder Pier Giorgio's virtues, take an inventory of your own life, and examine the ways you are feeling called to put your faith into action. At the end of each chapter, you'll find journal prompts to lead you in reflection and challenges to jump-start your growth as a person willing to put the Gospel into action.

Eight Days?

So why eight days for this retreat? Numbers often have significance in the biblical worldview. In his Sermon on the Mount (Mt 5:3–12), Christ gave us eight beatitudes, which radically overturn our expectations for what constitutes a "happy life." St. John Paul II called Pier Giorgio a "Man of the Beatitudes," for he radically lived out Jesus's call to be pure of heart, fight for righteousness, serve as a peacemaker, and be poor in spirit with a meek and humble heart.

Our faith tradition also sees eight as a number signifying the joy of new life. The earliest Christians thought of the moment of Christ's Resurrection as the first day of a new creation; if God created the world in seven days, Easter Sunday was the eighth. The eighth day—the Lord's day—signals the start of something new, so it seems fitting to encounter Pier Giorgio's exuberant joy over the course of eight days so we can start to practice his "newness of life" in play, friendship, prayer, and service.

Lastly, there is also a tradition stemming from the life of St. Ignatius of Loyola, the founder of the Society of Jesus (also known as the Jesuits). Ignatius led his followers on an intensive thirty-day retreat called the Spiritual Exercises, and he made modifications for an eight-day format that followed the same themes and flow. I've been blessed to participate in such Ignatian retreats, and I have experienced great fruit born from these times of prayer and reflection. I hope the eight days of this retreat with Frassati also bear great fruit in your life!

Befriending Frassati

As you venture ahead, I hope that you are encouraged by the example of this young man who lived a life fully alive before he was called to heaven at the age of twenty-four. We shouldn't fear giving our energies to God (however young or old we are), for he can transform all of our limited and meager efforts into something beautiful for others.

One of the enduring attributes of Frassati is his "ordinary" holiness. He wasn't a hermit or mountaintop mystic or prolific pope—he was a young student. He played pranks on his friends, he fell in love, he struggled to study, he loved to horse around—*and* he prioritized his relationship with Jesus Christ. He is a great example of what the Church calls the "universal call to holiness," which affirms that everyone—priest, nun, mother, businessman, student—can be transformed by God's grace to become a saint.

Learning and praying with Frassati over the course of writing this book has been a moving experience, especially because I recognize in his life some elements of my own. Like him, I also love the outdoors and the adventure of challenging physical experiences (I even worked as a firefighter briefly.) I experienced a wake-up call to my cradle-Catholic faith in my late-teen years and have been blessed by a long and maturing (and challenging!) friendship with the Lord. Over the last twenty years I have worked in a variety of ministries, such as teaching at an all-boy's Catholic school, parish roles and online evangelization, and working as a certified mentor with the CatholicPsych Institute. Frassati's story resonates in a deep way with the college students and young adults I know because he shows a way through that unique and restless time of life when we are seeking our calling and open to grand adventure, wherever the trail leads. He was a young man who soaked up the whole of life in a Christ-centered way and gave of himself to the last breath.

Maybe you are familiar with the story of Pier Giorgio and well-versed in the details of his life. Maybe you are curious and open to learning what is so endearing about this affable mountaineer, a figure who continues to inspire men and women globally. Perhaps you're at a crossroads in life, and you are feeling the full weight of life, with all its choices and burdens. Take heart, for you are right where God wants you to be, and you have not been forgotten. What's more, the life and words of Pier Giorgio Frassati just might be what you need to regain your footing and resume the climb before you.

Verso l'alto! To the heights!

Bobby Angel
November 1, 2024
Feast of All Saints

Fully Alive

Virtue of the Day: Courage

When you hear that someone is a saint, what do you imagine?

Someone unrelatable? A person who has never made a mistake and forever holds their hands in pious prayer? A strange desert hermit or a levitating monk? A nun locked away in a cloister, living a life of repetition and boredom? A person silently and scornfully judging everyone around them? A person who never sinned or can't possibly understand the modern struggles you're experiencing?

You wouldn't be alone in these assessments. Many Christians have looked to the holy men and women throughout the history of the faith, seeing them immortalized in marble or looking toward heaven on a prayer card, and have found the saints unapproachable, dry, or too otherworldly to have a realistic relationship with.

Take heart! These caricatures are a far cry from the reality of the gritty, flesh-and-blood soldiers of sanctity. The Church is full of colorful characters who came from all sorts of imperfect backgrounds, each with their own unique gifts, talents, temperaments, and afflictions.

Consider the dynamism within this short list of canonized saints: St. Peter and his brother Andrew were fishermen, prone to impulsivity—Peter even denied Jesus in his hour of need; St. Paul hunted down and murdered the early Christians before having a radical conversion and becoming a witness to the truth of the faith; St. Mary Magdalene had seven demons cast out of her and turned from a wayward life to devotion to the Lord, accompanying him through his death and to his Resurrection; St. Mark Ji Tianxiang was a doctor and opium addict who died by persecution in the Boxer Rebellion; St. Zelie Martin was a self-employed wife and mother who suffered and died from breast cancer at the end of the nineteenth century.

What the saints have in common is not a life lived without mistakes or sin (only Jesus and Mary can claim that title), but their commitment to turn *back* to God every time they stumble. Saints are Christians who don't give up. They allow the Lord to transform their lives—in the unique time period in which they all lived—for God's greater glory and for the conversion of others.

The Church is constantly recognizing men and women *even in our own times*—those who knew both the distractions and trials of our digital age and also the deep, transforming friendship of Jesus Christ. Just think of St. Carlo Acutis (1991–2006), an Italian teen and computer programmer who died of advanced leukemia, and Sr. Clare Crockett (1982–2016), a former actress and religious sister from Northern Ireland.

And we also have the humble, heroic example of Pier Giorgio Frassati.

Pier Giorgio Michelangelo Frassati was born on April 6, 1901, in the city of Turin, Italy. He lived a quiet but devout life, attending to his studies and being a generous friend. He climbed mountains and involved himself in political work. His life, cut tragically short at the age of twenty-four, wasn't anything extravagant when viewed from the outside, but on a closer look, it is apparent that his joy and service came through an intimate connection to the source of abundant life, which is Christ himself.

One of the alluring features of Pier Giorgio is his approachability. He was neither a dour-faced stoic nor an aloof intellectual. He was a student, an athlete, a prankster, and a young man responding to the call of living fully alive in Christ. A man described by Bishop Thomas Olmsted as "devout but not dainty, prayerful but not 'holier than thou,' and charitable and wholly committed to the truths of the Catholic faith."[1]

When his portrait was unveiled in St. Peter's Square during his beatification ceremony in 1990, the crowd witnessed the image of a dynamic young man atop a mountain peak, pickax in hand. This was no prudish figure or hidden-away recluse, not an unrelatable friar who lived a millennia ago and is now stoically encased in marble.

This was a man of action.

And now this man, Pier Giorgio Frassati, one hundred years after his death, is recognized as an official *saint* of the Catholic Church.

When you think of a saint, what are the first three names that come to mind? Which saints or heroic men and women in history do you feel closest to, and why?

To Be Fully Alive

The word "mediocre" comes from an infusion of two ancient words: *medius*, Latin for "middle," and *ocris*, which is an Old Latin word for "rugged mountain." To be mediocre is to literally be halfway up the mountain, neither at the bottom nor at the top.

Now, mediocrity might be a state we find ourselves in—mediocre in our guitar skills, job competency, or communication ability—but we should remember that we've simply reached a midpoint on our journey, not a final destination. Some of us will come to terms with persistent mediocrity in certain skills (like me in learning foreign languages or singing on key); we can't be excellent at everything, and that in itself is an important and humbling lesson to learn.

But perhaps as you've engaged in the climb of life, you've gotten "stuck" somehow. You might feel trapped by the circumstances of life, or beaten down by what you've endured. Perhaps you're constantly stressed and in perpetual "fight or flight" mode, or simply overwhelmed like a ship tossed about at sea. You're stuck in the middle of the mountain.

Experiences like this are part of the human condition. We get stuck in routines, feel uninspired by drabby workplaces, and sometimes struggle in unhealthy relationships. The new responsibilities of adulthood can have a dulling effect on the vibrancy and wonder for which we are made.

But deep in the human heart there is a pang that yearns for greatness. As Pope Benedict XVI said, "[We] were created for something great, for infinity. Nothing else will ever be enough. Saint Augustine was right when he said 'our hearts are restless till they find their rest in you.' The desire for a more meaningful life is a sign that God created us and that we bear his 'imprint.'"[2]

St. John Paul II explained more when he said, "It is Jesus who stirs in you the desire to do something great with your lives, the will to follow an ideal, the refusal to allow yourselves to be grounded down by mediocrity, the courage to commit yourselves humbly and patiently to improving yourselves and society, making the world more human and more fraternal."[3]

We don't set out to live "average" lives when we're young. We are hungry to live, to discover the world, and to test ourselves. We don't strive for mediocrity. We want to do something worthwhile with our lives, and that is a God-given call upon our hearts.

"The glory of God is man fully alive!" wrote St. Irenaeus, a bishop of the second century in what is modern-day France. To be a disciple is to say yes to a great adventure! We're not called to a life of shabbiness and boredom, or to become a marble statue as a copy of someone else. We're called to be fully *alive*, in the fullness of all that entails: the trials, the victories, the losses and heartbreaks, the times of waiting, the reaping of our hard work, the quiet moments of peace, the tender looks of love, and the offering of gifts from the heart. The first chapter of the *Catechism of the Catholic Church* puts it this way:

> The desire for God is written in the human heart because man is created by God and for God; and God never ceases to draw man to himself. Only in God will he find the truth and happiness he never stops searching for. . . . For if man exists, it is because God has created him through love, and through love continues to hold him in existence. (*CCC*, 27)

The revelation of God in human history, especially through the person of Jesus Christ, profoundly changed everything. Jesus did not come to give us rules and make us miserable, but to offer us new life—and life in abundance (Jn 10:10). The Christian faith is not a mere moral code but a grand love story. The God of the universe has known, loved, and called each one of us into being, into existence. When our hearts are open to receiving that encounter (not just the head knowledge that could give the right answer on a theology test), *nothing* remains the same. Every tender touch, every new morning and drop of rain, every interaction with another person is different.

When we fall in love with God, like Pier Giorgio Frassati did, *everything* changes.

Do you think you are living life "fully alive"? Why or why not? What is getting in the way of living with vibrance and boldness?

.   .   .   .

.   .   .   .

To Jesus, Through Frassati

When it comes to pursuing God and his plan for our lives, shouldn't we simply focus on Christ alone? Why bother with the saints, with Mary, or with any other intermediary—even Pier Giorgio?

Of course, we can and *should* go to Jesus without delay or fear; he knows our hearts, our sins, and our wounds, and he is pouring out his mercy upon us every day. He is the one who laid down his life for our sins, and through faith in him we have eternal life (Jn 3:16).

But God also calls us into communion—that is, relationship with one another. We do not exist in solitudes or as "lone rangers"; we are meant to be a part of the bigger Body of Christ, the Church. And this Church, we believe, doesn't solely exist in the members here on earth but also those in the life to come.

Just as I would ask a family member or friend to pray for me, we look to the saints with the same request. Though they have departed from this Earth, they are *alive* in Christ, and thus are closely intimate with him and able to intercede on our behalf.

What's more, many of us might be aware that we're not entirely worthy (no one is, of course!) or comfortable going directly to Jesus. We can feel burdened by shame or guilt, or perhaps just don't find Jesus "relatable" enough to approach him within our prayer. Here, too, is where God graciously gives us the greater Body of Christ to be our companions on the journey.

Maybe we feel more affinity with St. Josephine Bakhita or St. Thérèse of Lisieux, so we ask for their prayers to encourage us on our walk of faith. Or when we feel burdened by obstacles and scrupulosity, we might ask for the intercession of St. Thomas More or St. Maximilian Kolbe. In the same vein, the purpose of this book is to foster a growing connection with Pier Giorgio Frassati so you can invite him to be your companion on the way toward the heart of Christ.

The twelfth-century monk and mystic St. Bernard of Clairvaux wrote on the value of looking to the saints, so it's worth quoting him at length:

> Calling the saints to mind inspires, or rather arouses in us, above all else, a longing to enjoy their company, so desirable in itself. We long to share in the citizenship of heaven, to dwell with the spirits of the blessed, to join the assembly of patriarchs, the ranks of the prophets, the council of apostles, the great host of martyrs, the noble company of confessors and the choir of virgins. In short, we long to be united in happiness with all the saints. But our dispositions change. The Church of all the first followers of Christ awaits us, but we do nothing about it. The saints want us to be with them, and we are indifferent. The souls of the just await us, and we ignore them.
>
> Come, brothers, let us at length spur ourselves on. We must rise again with Christ; we must seek the world which is above and set our minds on the things of heaven. Let us long for those who are longing for

us, hasten to those who are waiting for us, and ask
those who look for our coming to intercede for us.
We should not only want to be with the saints, but
we should also hope to possess their happiness. While
we desire to be in their company, we must also ear-
nestly seek to share in their glory. Do not imagine that
there is anything harmful in such an ambition as this;
there is no danger in setting our hearts on such glory.
When we commemorate the saints we are inflamed
with another yearning: that Christ our life may also
appear to us as he appeared to them and that we may
one day share in his glory.[4]

The saints never glory in themselves. They all point to
the fulfillment of our longings, the triune God. "We worship
Christ as God's Son; we love the martyrs as the Lord's disciples and imitators," wrote St. Polycarp, one of the early church
fathers.[5] Pier Giorgio Frassati does the same for us—by the
witness of his life, he reveals a path to the Trinity that travels
through mountaineering adventures, service to the poor, and
dedication to his friends.

*In the space below, sketch out what a life "fully alive" looks like
for you. What goals do you want to accomplish? What's your best
understanding of what you are being called to do with your life?
What is the thing that you are most afraid of doing? Why does it
cause you fear?*

.   .   .   .

.   .   .   .

Leap into Action

Start a conversation with a close friend about greatness. Consider using the following suggested structure:

- First, spend some time contemplating what your ambitions are—what do you aspire to?

- Second, reflect on what this ambition will require of your character and spiritual life.

- Finally, open a dialogue with a good friend about what greatness might look like for each of you. Begin the conversation by telling your friend a little bit about Frassati and how his life made you start thinking about what you wanted to do with your life.

Pray

God our Father, thank you for calling me to know, love, and serve you. You have given me a unique place in the Body of Christ. Help me to know that I am not alone, even if I find myself in a place of struggle or trial. With the intercession of Pier Giorgio Frassati, grant me the grace to put into action the challenge of living a vibrant and full life of self-gift in imitation of your Son, Jesus Christ. Amen!

The Mountains Are Calling

Virtues of the Day: Excellence and Wonder

Adventurous and athletic from his early youth, Pier Giorgio loved the challenge of the mountains. He told a friend once that he left his heart on a mountaintop and looked forward to retrieving it on a climb to the summit of Mont Blanc.[1]

As a member of the Italian Alpine Club, he climbed the Gran Tournalin (11,086 ft.), the Grivola in the Val d'Aosta (13,022 ft.), Mon Viso (12,602 ft.), the Ciamarella (12,060 ft.), and the Bessanese (11,588 ft.).[2] Frassati loved the challenge of physical exertion and pushing his body and soul to their maximum potential. Photos abound of him perched above the peaks and assisting friends in these expeditions. This was also the era of much more rudimentary climbing gear; Frassati and his companions looked quite rugged (and dapper) in their period clothing compared with today's neon, insulated, and synthetic apparel donned by climbers decked out with air tanks and specialized equipment.

"Every day that passes, I fall more desperately in love with the mountains," Frassati wrote. "I am ever more determined to climb the mountains, to scale the mighty peaks, to feel that pure joy which can only be felt in the mountains."[3] He climbed his last mountain on June 7, 1925, and a now-famous photo of him climbing on his final ascent bears his own handwritten caption: *Verso l'alto*—to the heights!

Whether we are avid outdoor adventurers or not, we all feel pulled to search for the heights of human experience and pursue excellence. There is a sense of "dialing in" when you're pressed up against a rock face, swimming in the waves of the ocean, running a race, or tumbling down a white-water rapid. Every sense in the body needs to be activated to skillfully succeed (or survive) these kinds of endeavors.

When we find ourselves completely absorbed in a particular activity and flooded with mood-enhancing chemicals, we experience the hours flying by in minutes—a phenomenon that researchers call a "flow state." The activities and hobbies that consume us capture our attention, and we lose track of time engaging in them. This could be writing, dancing, playing music, praying, or climbing a sheer rock face.

Alex Honnold, the climber highlighted in the documentary *Free Solo* (which showcased his climb of El Capitan at Yosemite *without a rope* in record time), affirms that he doesn't have a death wish and isn't an adrenaline junkie—he's simply seeking *excellence*. "When climbing feels good, when it feels effortless, when it feels flowy. That's the flow state," Honnold notes. "And that is the appeal of climbing, in a lot of ways, to get into that state. To feel like you're doing something well and that you're performing well."[4]

Excellence—it's our human calling to pursue the *heights* of living, and there's no better place to test ourselves than letting us be challenged by the outdoors, where we are surrounded by the majesty of creation.

When did you last feel fully immersed in an activity that you loved? What activity or hobby brings new life to you? How might you spend more time pursuing excellence for its own sake, just because doing hard things well is fun?

Finding Meaning in the Mountains

St. Pope John Paul II was an avid skier and loved stealing away into the mountains—at one of his addresses, he explained why:

> Every time I can go to the mountains and contemplate this scenery, I thank God for the majestic beauty of creation. I thank him for his own beauty, of which the universe is a reflection capable of stirring attentive hearts and prompting them to praise his greatness. A mountain, in particular, is not only a magnificent scene to contemplate but a school of life as it were. In this school we learn to strive for a goal and to help one another in difficult moments, to enjoy silence together and to recognize one's own littleness in so solemn and majestic a setting.[5]

The *Catechism of the Catholic Church* teaches that there is a "solidarity among all creatures arising from the fact that all have the same Creator," and "the beauty of creation reflects the infinite beauty of the Creator and ought to inspire the respect and submission of man's intellect and will" (*CCC*, 341, 344). Nature, rightly examined, can lead us into deeper contemplation and gratitude for our connection to our Creator.

The danger is when our hearts are tempted to worship the mountains, to give our highest praise to creation rather than the Creator. Nature is an impersonal force: its waters can nourish just as quickly as they can drown, and the mountains can take life just as quickly as they can inspire life. Animals that are majestic to admire can turn via cold instinct to trample or kill.

Professor and philosopher Peter Kreeft writes, "Do not worship even the biggest, most beautiful thing on earth, the sea. Only God is God. Do not confuse the finite with the Infinite. And the sea has no morality. It kills. It steals. It deceives. It dishonors. It will wash away your sorrows, and it will wash away your shallowness, but it will not wash away your sins."[6]

Knowing the dangers and risks of mountaineering, Frassati also noted how nature surely puts us in contact with our own mortality. "When one goes into the mountains one should sort out one's conscience, because one never knows if one will come home," he wrote. "But despite all this, I am not afraid, and on the contrary I want to climb the mountains more than ever, to conquer the most daring peaks; to feel that pure joy, which one can only have in the mountains."[7]

Discernment is required here, of course. Frassati wasn't reckless, but he also did not let risk prevent him from experiencing what this world had to offer. We can't heedlessly throw ourselves into danger because the natural world can be unforgiving. But it's also true that we are tempted to the path of least resistance—whether that's on a hike, or in the dynamics of a personal relationship. What heights might we be missing by not challenging ourselves to explore beyond our comfort zones?

Safetism is the pervading sense that we can control all outcomes and eliminate all risks. Such a "safety first" mindset is not only false (simply stepping outside the door entails risk), but this mindset also leads to a life not worth living. To attempt to exist in a sanitized bubble without any hint of danger robs us of our potential for growth. Many of our tendencies toward avoiding discomfort or pain may seemingly have short-term benefits, but they rob us of the long-term fruit when we are mature enough to push our limits to become the men and women we're called to be.

Frassati embraced pushing past his limits whenever he began his ascents, soaking up both the challenges and the joys of his physical and spiritual climbs. He ventured forward and upward despite the risks and dangers, uncertain if he would succeed because he was reaching for greatness.

Where are you tempted to "play it safe"? When was the last time you stepped out into the challenge of the unknown? Where do you have opportunities to push beyond your comfort zone? Define "reach for greatness" for yourself—where might Frassati's spirit of adventure take you?

. . . .

. . . .

. . . .

. . . .

I Wonder as I Wander

"These alpine climbs have a strange magic in them so that no matter how many times they are repeated and however alike they are, they are never boring," Pier Giorgio wrote to his friend Tina Aimone-Catt, saying, "in the same way as the experience of spring is never boring but fills our spirit with gladness and delight."[8]

The ancient philosopher Socrates noted, through the writings of his student Plato, "Wonder is the beginning of wisdom." Being curious about the cosmos, how things work, why things are the way they are—these are all signs of an open mind and receptive heart. A child is naturally inquisitive and asks everything about everything. But as we grow older we often become closed off and perhaps jaded, no longer curious of the world. At worst, we can arrogantly think we know all that we need to know (or lethargically shrug off any need to ask questions because the internet has the answers to everything anyway).

It's so easy to lose the childlike eyes to notice and appreciate with wonder the miraculous beauty and interconnectedness of the world. What is required to recover this type of wonder are intentionality and attentiveness. Go on a walk without your phone, drive without listening to a podcast, slow down and notice the very breath that sustains us unconsciously every single moment. If we can regain a sense of curiosity about the world, we'll remember that there are always millions of more questions to be asked. And nothing jolts us back into a posture of wonder like the transcendent beauty of the created world—the mountains, seas, and stars.

"Every day I fall in love with the mountains more and more," Frassati wrote to a friend. "If my studies would allow me to do it, I would spend entire days on the mountains contemplating in that pure air the greatness of the creator."[9] Beauty strikes and arrests us—it stops us in our tracks. Whether it's an expansive landscape or peaceful sunset, an enchanting sonata or movie score, or the lovely face of our beloved, beauty is God's gift to us and is meant to awaken wonder.

It's even easy to lose a sense of wonder about ourselves—the mystery of our lives, our meaning and purpose. "People are moved to wonder by mountain peaks, by vast waves of the sea, by broad waterfalls on rivers, by the all-embracing extent of the ocean, by the revolutions of the stars. But in themselves they are uninterested,"[10] wrote St. Augustine, one of the Church's greatest thinkers.

The mountains and the whole of creation can shake us back to life like few other things can. Frassati knew this, and his zeal for this beauty challenges us to rediscover it for ourselves amid all our technology and creature comforts.

St. John Paul II famously loved the mountains for the same reasons Frassati did. He wrote about them in his Angelus address given on July 15, 2001:

With this amazing scenery before our eyes, I naturally think of the Psalms in which creation, and especially the mountains, comes to the fore.

I am thinking, for example, of Psalm 8: "O Lord, Our God", the Psalmist exclaims in Psalm 8, "how great is your name through all the earth" (vv. 2.10). In Ps 19 (18) we read "the heavens tell the glory of God; and the firmament proclaims his handiwork" (v. 2). In fact, creation is the first chapter of revelation that God entrusted to human minds and hearts.

Psalm 23 (22) says so splendidly, "the Lord is my shepherd . . . he makes me lie down in green pastures, he leads me beside still waters, he refreshes my soul. He leads me in the path of righteousness . . .".

The whole of Psalm 104 (103) is a hymn to the Creator: "bless the Lord, O my soul / O Lord my God, you are very great! / . . . You make the springs gush forth in the valleys / they flow between the hills; / . . . The high mountains are for the wild goats; the rocks are a refuge for the badgers. . . . O Lord how manifold are your works!" (vv. 1-2.5.8.10-11.18.24). We need to make these sentiments our own in the face of the natural beauty that is so awe-inspiring![11]

What parts of creation captivate your attention? Recall an immersive experience of the beauty of the natural world that stopped you in your tracks and led you to wonder at the majesty of creation. What sensory details can you remember about what that experience was like? Write them down and revisit that place in your memory and imagination. Linger there with gratitude.

.   .   .   .

.   .   .   .

.   .   .   .

.   .   .   .

Leap into Action

Unplug and find a spot in the natural world to practice wonder. Spend ten minutes or more noticing everything you can. Open all of your senses, not just sight. Stay open and curious, even to seemingly mundane details. Notice where your mind goes and what thoughts or questions arise. Give thanks to God for his creation.

Pray

Lord, grant me new eyes to see with childlike wonder the world you created and sustain. You placed humanity at the summit of your creation and invite us to participate in and steward it. With the intercession of Pier Giorgio Frassati, help me grow in my appreciation for the magnificent scale of your creation and my own humble significance within this vast universe as your beloved child. Amen!

DAY 3
The Host of Heaven

Virtue of the Day: Devotion

Pier Giorgio received his first Holy Communion on June 19, 1911, at the age of ten.

Pope Pius X, who took office when Pier Giorgio was two years old, encouraged the Christian faithful to receive Holy Communion often (daily, if possible), and he also asserted that children should receive the Eucharist earlier in life (around the age of reason, seven or eight years old, rather than the customary age of twelve).

These encouragements spurred on Frassati's devotion to the Lord, and he received the Eucharist almost daily until the day of his death. His sister Luciana wrote, "The power of Christ working in him every morning is the only explanation we can give to particular heroic acts of self-sacrifice and of charity, to his enormous spirit of humility, and to the moral astuteness of his life."[1]

Frassati would often steal away to visit the Blessed Sacrament in thanksgiving for his life and blessings, even before and after his mountain climbs. Sometimes he spent the night in a chapel wearing his mountaineering gear before leaving early the next morning.

The robustness of his life and faith might indicate that Pier Giorgio came from a devout and supportive family, but he was largely on his own in matters of religious practice. His father was an agnostic and did not attend Mass with the family. His mother considered religion a formality, a box to be checked for the sake of polite society, just as one must do their chores or pay their taxes. The thought of going beyond the bare minimum for Catholicism was scarcely considered in the Frassati household. And with the rising anti-clerical political unrest in Italy at the time, practicing one's faith also came with potential consequences. It is surely by the grace of God that, on top of the naturally virtuous character he already possessed, Frassati was guided by formators and priests at key moments of his upbringing so that he was able to dive deeply into the Catholic faith.

Largely due to his struggles with learning Latin, Pier Giorgio was sent to learn under the Jesuits and fit two years of study into one in order to make up for failing exams. Christine Wohar, author and founder of the FrassatiUSA apostolate, writes:

> And what if [he] might have excelled in Latin? What would have become of "his poor" if he had not been sent to the Jesuit school where he was introduced to the Conferences of St. Vincent de Paul? That academic struggle was such a source of embarrassment for him and his parents, but it became the springboard that took him to greater spiritual heights. . . . It is also a good reminder for us that life's disappointments are not always as bad or as permanent as they may at first seem.[2]

Some of us might identify with such an upbringing where religion serves as window-dressing and is not taken seriously. Frassati sought something deeper because what he found in Catholicism resonated with the deep ache of the human heart.

While we should certainly spend our energies helping those around us in need, the purpose of the Church (and the Christian life) is not solely charitable works, but the salvation of souls. We have an eternal destiny—God *wants* us to exist, and he yearns for us to spend eternity with him. This truth is mind-blowing if we dare to contemplate it. The origin and end of the universe—the Creator of heaven and earth—has written himself on our hearts and never ceases drawing us to himself (*CCC*, 27).

Through prayer and the sacraments, especially the Eucharist, we grow in union and conversation with Christ. The "effortless" faith of Pier Giorgio seemed so natural partly because he *spent time with the Lord* as a daily communicant. Some researchers say that it takes ten thousand hours to become an "expert" at something: golf, guitar, Mario Kart, etc. Whatever the number may be, in order to become a worthy student, spouse, or saint, it boils down to *putting in the time* with one's beloved. If we are to pursue joyful sanctity as men and women in Christ, we have to put in the time with the Lord. We can read and study *about* Jesus (and we should), but it's no substitute for being *with* him, especially receiving our Lord in every Mass or spending time in adoration of him in the Blessed Sacrament.

"Jesus comes to me every day in Holy Communion," Frassati affirmed. "I repay him in my miserable way by visiting the poor." As we'll see soon, the outpouring of Pier Giorgio's generosity started first in his daily encounter with Christ and the reception of his grace. From that divine relationship poured forth Frassati's work in serving others.

We can't give what we don't have. Pier Giorgio received Christ in a daily, intimate way through the Eucharist. That was the only fuel he needed.

In what ways do you treat faith as "window-dressing"? How can you more deeply encounter Jesus Christ as he comes to you in the Eucharist and in the world? What difference does Jesus's presence in the Eucharist make in your life?

God Is Good

When you think of God, what do you imagine? What is the portrait of God that best reflects your relationship with him? We get many different images of God from religion and culture—from a loving Father, to a just judge, to a genie, to a police officer, to an old man with a beard who lives in the clouds. Some of these images align with what we know of God through our tradition of faith, and some don't help at all.

For example, our Christian faith is not one that claims we should cower in fear before a tyrant God; we don't believe that we have license to do anything as though the Almighty were a fun uncle; we don't see the Lord as a cosmic Santa Claus who only exists to reward us if we are good; nor ought we feel aimless and uncared for as if God were an impersonal creator who couldn't be bothered with us. These misconceptions are all too common in our culture, and they misrepresent the God who has revealed himself in our history through the story of salvation—from Abraham, Isaac, and Jacob, to the full revelation of himself in the person of Jesus Christ.

God is a mystery revealed to us as a communion of persons. The Trinity—Father, Son, and Holy Spirit—is an eternal exchange of love, and we are *destined* to take part in that exchange. This is life-changing stuff if we stop to take it in! We are made for union and communion because we have been created in the image and likeness of this Trinitarian God. We see this theological truth play out in our lives every day: we are built for relationship and only find meaning and purpose for our lives through love.

At the same time, we don't always live out of this truth—wounds, traumas, sins, indifferences, or hardness of heart can get in the way. We may think of God as an intellectual problem to be solved (i.e., trying to prove God's existence) or an authority figure to be reckoned with rather than a person beckoning us into union with him.

Pier Giorgio's faith flowed from a deep sense of the goodness of God and love of Jesus Christ. He judged no one but was pained by those hypocritical in their behavior, his contemporaries who attended Mass out of mechanical duty and indulged in behaviors contrary to that of a disciple of Christ. The Eucharist for Pier Giorgio was a supreme gift, not an obligation, and it pained him when he heard someone roll their eyes and say, "Tomorrow I *have* to go to Mass." For Frassati, this was a lack of respect toward the living God. Worshipping God on holy days and Sundays was an *opportunity*, not an obligation. But we can only understand this disposition if our faith is a divine love story, not an oppressing moral code.

God actually does love *you*, dear reader; he delights in you, and he desires for you to see him face-to-face.

How do you envision God? What are the operative images of God that define your relationship with him? What images of God from scripture and tradition might challenge your portrait of who God is?

The Host of Heaven

Complementing Pier Giorgio's unwavering devotion to Christ in the Blessed Sacrament was his veneration of the host of the Church triumphant in heaven, the saints—especially the honor and praise he gave to Mary.

Pier Giorgio wrote often of Mary, entrusting his friends to her care, and joined confraternities such as the Society of the Rosary and the Soldiers of Mary. A rosary was with him at all times—as he noted to a friend, "I carry my testament in my pocket."[3] He would pray the Rosary publicly and invited strangers to join him as he thumbed the beads. Against the accusation that he had become a "fanatic," he would simply answer, "No, I have remained a Christian."[4]

Pier Giorgio understood the safe refuge that Mary provided. His friend Marco Beltramo wrote, "We can't understand the spirituality of Pier Giorgio if we don't understand his love for the Blessed Virgin Mary." According to his sister, Frassati consecrated himself to Mary at the age of seventeen years old.[5]

He would take part in Marian processions in the streets of Turin, often holding the canopy pole over the statue of the Virgin. At a time when both Communists and Fascists were becoming increasingly aggressive, to take part in a public religious procession often risked altercation or injury. His friend Marco noted that "the surest means by which Pier Giorgio achieved his union with the Lord, the secret of his spiritual perfection, was his total devotion to Mary."[6]

Pier Giorgio also felt inspired by St. Dominic, the founder of the Dominican Order and the saint through whom Mary gave us the devotion of the Rosary. The Dominican charism of prayer and preaching attracted him, and he loved the writings of St. Catherine of Siena. Like her, he joined the Lay Dominicans and became a "Third Order" member, taking the name Girolamo after a Renaissance preacher who experienced great persecution.

Frassati likewise held in high esteem St. Paul for his courage and zeal for preaching the Gospel. "There is a lack of peace in the world which has distanced itself from God," he wrote to his friend Marco, "but there is also a lack of charity; that is, true and perfect Love. Maybe if all of us listened more to St. Paul, human miseries would be slightly diminished."[7]

Pier Giorgio put together an all-star team in heaven—a community of friends he looked up to and asked for help. Mary, Paul, Catherine, and Dominic were saints who inspired him to deeper faithfulness and higher virtue. This is who the saints are for us, as well; their heroic witness calls us to more, and they are cheering us on from heaven, ready to intercede for us if we need their help.

Who inspires you, and why? What leaders, saints, or people in your life help you to desire to be better? Who do you believe is cheering you on in life right now—on earth and in heaven?

The Eucharistic Fire

We've learned about Frassati's devotion to the Eucharist, his faith in God's goodness, and the way he saw himself as part of a communion of people seeking holiness. His was a rightly ordered heart; he trained his desires to find their end and fulfillment in God, and he relished opportunities to nourish and deepen that relationship, whether it was in the beauty of the mountains or praying the Rosary. "Every now and then I ask myself: shall I go on trying to follow the right path? Will

I have the good fortune to persevere to the end?" he wrote. "In this tremendous clash of doubts, the faith given to me in baptism suggests to me with a sure voice, 'By yourself you can do nothing, but if you have God as the center of your every action, then, yes, you will reach the goal.'"[8]

Frassati knew that faith was, first and foremost, a relationship with God, and that this relationship opened up a new world to him, one full of truth, beauty, and goodness that could not be found anywhere else. He practiced faith not out of a dry sense of duty or because he was unthinkingly obedient—he prayed and served out of love. He wanted to grow in intimacy with God, and he took advantage of all the ways God reveals himself to us, especially in his Son, Jesus, and the Church he founded. In a beautifully written speech to the Catholic Youth of Pollone, Frassati wrote:

> I urge you with all the strength of my soul to approach the Eucharistic Table as often as possible. Feed on this Bread of the Angels from which you will draw the strength to fight inner struggles, the struggles against passions and against all adversaries, because Jesus Christ has promised to those who feed themselves with the most Holy Eucharist, eternal life and the necessary graces to obtain it. And when you become totally consumed by the Eucharistic Fire, then you will be able to thank with greater awareness the Lord God who has called you to be part of his flock and you will enjoy that peace which those who are happy according to the world have never tasted. Because true happiness, young people, does not consist in the pleasures of the world and in earthly things, but in peace

of conscience which we can have only if we are pure in heart and in mind.[9]

What we worship is what we give our highest "worth" to. When they have an oversized hold on our desires, even good things can take the first priority of value in our lives, when only God can satisfy. Taking an objective and candid look at your life, what desires displace your desire for God? What are the things that have an oversized hold on your heart? Where are you tempted to idolize or worship things other than God (nature, family, relationships, money, popularity or status, pleasure, etc.)?

Leap into Action

Make the time to pray—for real. Set a timer on your phone for ten or fifteen minutes, and start with quiet, unstructured prayer in which you speak to God from the heart about where you hope he will lead you in this journey with Frassati. From there, spend the rest of the time in quiet contemplation, praying the Rosary, or reading the Bible. If you feel called to more, make a plan to attend daily Mass.

Pray

Lord, help me to see with clarity the things I prize instead of you. Purify my intentions and untangle my distorted desires. Allow me to worship you alone. With the aid of Pier Giorgio, allow me to put my hand to the work you have given me, to not look back, and to move forward with growing trust in your mercy and guidance. Amen!

DAY 4
The Cheerful Giver

Virtue of the Day: Generosity

A knock came at the door of the Frassati home when Pier Giorgio was four years old. A ragged woman stood there with an equally impoverished child in tow. Noticing the child's bare feet, Pier Giorgio took off his own shoes and socks and handed them to her and quickly shut the door, worried his family would disapprovingly see the situation.

This wasn't an isolated incident. His whole life was marked by a spontaneous generosity and a heart moved for the poor. From a remarkably young age, he had the ability to see Christ in others and to give without counting the cost. Frassati recognized this solidarity as simply the right thing to do: "Jesus Christ has promised that all we do for the poor for love of him he will consider it as having been done to himself," he wrote.[1]

Frassati kept a notebook that held the addresses of people in need. He would frequently visit these men and women, bringing rations of food or clothing and offering his warm presence. To his dying breath, Pier Giorgio had on his mind and heart those who lived on the margins—even on his deathbed, he scribbled out a note to direct a friend in the Conference of St. Vincent de Paul to bring medicine to a local impoverished man.

When Frassati's family spent time abroad during his father's tenure as the Italian ambassador to Germany, the poor of their new country were his companions. He would take the flowers from the Italian embassy's office and place them on the graves of the poor, and once he gave away his winter coat to a beggar on the street. "With every day that passes, I fall more and more in love with the Germans," Frassati wrote, and when he learned that his family would return to Italy, he left a letter for a local friend with money enclosed, writing: "I wanted to do so much for the Germans, but unfortunately there is nothing I can do. Please take this money for the poor children of Berlin. It isn't much, but I guess it is better than nothing."[2]

"He considered himself to be the administrator of a treasure that did not belong to him, of which he would have to give an account one day," wrote Luciana on her brother's attitude toward money. "That is why he could not bear avarice or waste."[3]

"The face of God revealed by Jesus is that of a Father concerned for and close to the poor," Pope Francis noted in a 2021 address. The pope continued:

> This is a summons never to lose sight of every opportunity to do good. Behind it, we can glimpse the ancient biblical command: 'If one of your brothers and sisters . . . is in need, you shall not harden your heart nor close your hand to them in their need. Instead, you shall open your hand to them and freely lend them enough to meet their need. . . . When you give to them, give freely and not with ill will; for the Lord, your God, will bless you for this in all your works and

undertakings. For the needy will never be lacking in the land . . .' (Deut 15:7–8, 10–11). In a similar vein, the Apostle Paul urged the Christians of his communities to come to the aid of the poor of the first community of Jerusalem and to do so 'without sadness or compulsion, for God loves a cheerful giver' (2 Cor 9:7). It is not a question of easing our conscience by giving alms, but of opposing the culture of indifference and injustice we have created with regard to the poor.[4]

Who are the people in need living in close proximity to you—in your city and on your streets? What do they need the most, and how can you offer your time, talent, or treasure to respond to them? How can you offer the gift of friendship in addition to material help?

Fighting Injustice

Italy at the turn of the twentieth century was in disarray. After a long period of ruling factions and city-states, Italy became one unified country in 1861 (Rome was named its capital in 1871.) But large swaths of Italy, particularly the southern regions, were in poverty, and the government was perceived as untrustworthy. Leaders were assassinated, and millions of

Italians fled to other countries (including the United States) beginning in the late 1800s through the early 1900s.

The Italy that the Frassati family knew teemed with strife and political uncertainties. As the Bolshevik Revolution began overtaking the Russian landscape and sowing seeds of Communism in the eastern regions of Europe, movements of fascism began to take root in nations to the West—most notably Italy and Germany.

In 1922, thousands of fascists were marching on Rome. Soon after, they seized control of the government—the charismatic leader Benito Mussolini, through manipulation and schemes of violence, became the *de facto* dictator of Italy by 1925.

With his eyes open to the abounding injustices, Frassati found it difficult to keep a low profile at times. He frequently spoke his mind, which was against the prevailing wisdom to keep one's head down and not ruffle the feathers of the new regime. "With violence you sow hatred, and you harvest its bad fruits," Frassati asserted. "With charity, you sow peace among men—not the peace the world gives, but the true peace that only faith in Jesus Christ can give us in common brotherhood."

Frassati noted, "I am still trying to make sense of the violence the Communists have caused in some countries," and he was especially frustrated by the tactics of the fascist thugs he encountered on a regular basis in his home country. He was even attacked when a batch of men broke into his home.[5] Before anyone in his family was injured, he bravely chased them out of his house and down the street, landing a punch and calling them cowards as they fled.

Frassati, like Christ himself, was slow to anger, but he was moved by injustice to righteous outrage. He joined numerous community groups and was outspoken at rallies that called for greater accountability from government officials, always keeping his eyes on Christ as the model of self-possession to avoid becoming absorbed in a mob mentality. An acquaintance noted how, "during the most heated debates . . . Pier Giorgio went out of his way to show respect and kindness to his opponent, as if to show that he was fighting an idea, not the individual."[6]

We won't achieve utopia on this side of heaven. Pier Giorgio knew this well, understanding that ultimate justice only awaits us in the next life, but that didn't stop him from trying to make his society better to the extent that he could. He made an effort to faithfully form his conscience, the place where God's voice speaks in every human heart, and followed the convictions he felt there, no matter if they were unpopular or risky. "It is better to stand alone, but with a clean conscience," Frassati wrote, "than to stand with all the rest, but with a giant stain on our conscience."[7]

What cultural or political issues are important to you—and why? What issues deserve more or less of your attention? In what areas does your conscience need formation? What are the sources you listen to when forming conclusions about the world? How do those voices align with the guidance we get from our bishops and the pope and the catechism? How can you step out of your bubble to better encounter, understand, and engage with opinions and worldviews that differ from your own? How can you grow in your advocacy for justice?

. . . .

. . . .

. . . .

. . . .

Moved by Solidarity

Compassion for people living in poverty moved Pier Giorgio to the point he wished to be constantly among them. When asked why he often rode in third-class cabins on trains, he answered that there was no fourth class. It wasn't enough to donate to a third-party organization and feel as if he had done his part—Frassati needed to share life with those on the margins.

In Jesus's time, leprosy was a chronic bacterial infection that attacked the skin and various parts of the body. It was understood to be a sign of one's cursedness. No one wanted anything to do with a leper—they were forbidden to be touched and were subjected to rigorous examination (Lv 13–14). As a result, lepers were often cast out of society—they were literal outsiders.

With radical compassion, Jesus touched and cleansed those infected with leprosy (Mk 1:40–42); he healed ten lepers who came to him all at once (Lk 17:11–19). Today, leprosy is known as Hansen's disease and is considered treatable, but there are still many outsiders who are excluded from our networks and circles.

There are many ways people are marginalized, whether because of material poverty, racism, prejudice, disability, or any number of other factors. A deeper reality of loneliness and isolation runs through all forms of exclusion, which is the greatest poverty. Mother Teresa, in a passage from her profound work *A Simple Path*, explains:

> The greatest disease in the West today is not TB or leprosy; it is being unwanted, unloved, and uncared for. We can cure physical diseases with medicine, but the only cure for loneliness, despair, and hopelessness is love. There are many in the world who are dying for a piece of bread but there are many more dying for a little love. The poverty in the West is a different kind of poverty—it is not only a poverty of loneliness but also of spirituality. There's a hunger for love, as there is a hunger for God.[8]

When enthusiastic would-be missionaries volunteered to join her, Mother Teresa would say, "Find your own Calcutta." We don't need to venture to the other side of the world to serve; there are people in need around us wherever we are. Frassati met the needs of those around him, whether he was in Turin, in Germany, or on a mountain slope with friends.

Who is someone in your circle or network or community who lacks what they need to flourish—who needs material assistance or (more importantly) friendship? How might you be able to offer your compassion and attention to them? What holds you back from being more detached with your possessions, finances, or time? How might you grow in your trust that God will provide you with what you need if you share what you have?

Leap into Action

Step outside of your comfort zone to be generous with your time, talent, or treasure toward those in need. Find a ministry or nonprofit who could use assistance, and see how you might contribute—even if it's for a limited amount of time. Focus on relationship and solidarity over "making an impact," and discover what gifts those on the margins have to offer.

Pray

Lord Jesus, help me to become a peacemaker and to seek justice with zeal. Expand my heart so that I may be slow to anger and moved with compassion for all I meet. Through the intercession of Pier Giorgio, reveal to me the ways I can alleviate the suffering of others around me, and grant me the courage to act decisively for those who need a sign of your love. Amen!

DAY 5
Fraternity and Family

Virtue of the Day: Loyalty

Laughing, smiling, mischief, play. If you glance through the existing photos we have of Pier Giorgio, you will see a young man constantly smiling wide in the embrace of friends. From university gatherings, to hiking trips, to political participation, Frassati embodied an outward-oriented disposition—he had a willingness to engage with anyone God put in his life, and he sought to draw them to the Lord, the source of his joy.

As a college student, he and a group of friends created a club called the *Tipi Loschi* ("the Shady Characters"). We can read in their letters lots of friendly teasing, frivolity, and jokes (Pier Giorgio playfully took the name Robespierre, after the French radical), but the group's deeper purpose was to support one another in recreation and in prayer. They would also poke fun through satire at the serious issues of their day, such as rising fascism and censorship in Italian culture.

On his mountaintop excursions, Frassati would always have a watchful eye over those who were struggling to make the climb. Sometimes he pretended his foot hurt so that the group would stop and rest for the sake of not humiliating an individual who lagged behind, and he was always quick to help carry the gear of those who were growing tired.

He enjoyed hanging out and playing billiards with friends. The pool table they were using broke, which led to a dispute between Frassati and a repairman who was trying to take advantage of their group. Why was playing pool important to Frassati? Having a functioning billiards table at the university meant that his peers would be more apt to stay on campus than to frequent the bars of Turin. He would also make wagers with classmates, betting that if he won, the loser would accompany him to Mass, adoration, or some other spiritual devotion.

Frassati certainly enjoyed play for the sake of play, but he never missed an opportunity to push others toward deeper relationship with the Lord. He also didn't miss a chance to sing, despite the fact that he was often off-key and didn't possess the highest quality voice. "Singing is a lover's thing," noted St. Augustine, explaining that only the one who is in love doesn't care for the self-preservation of trying to save face. A lover puts his or her voice out there vulnerably to express themselves to their beloved.

Who is the friend who has had the deepest impact on your life? How have they inspired joy or challenged you? Jot some thoughts here about how they have changed your life.

Faithful to Family

One of the most relatable dimensions of Pier Giorgio's life was the way he loved his family, particularly in the midst of navigating their woundedness and disapproval of his Christ-centered way of life.

Pier Giorgio and his younger sister, Luciana, actually had an older sister, but she died in infancy. His parents, Adelaide and Alfredo, had a tumultuous marriage—both were absorbed in their own work and the demands of their stations in high society. In the later years, they were on the brink of separation, and their unhappiness often spilled over into the rest of the family.

Both parents were hesitant and even antagonistic about Pier Giorgio's deepening faith, considering his piety and devotion too "radical." His daily reception of Communion was misunderstood by his family, and he often hid his charitable actions from his parents. When a nun asked Adelaide about the possibility of her son becoming a priest, she responded, "I would rather he graduate from the university and die."[1]

Pier Giorgio never seriously discerned at length the possibility of becoming a priest for the sake of not causing his parents further distress and so he could be hands-on with the people of Italy. To please his father, he later in life agreed to serve on the administration of *La Stampa* once his studies were finished, even though he had hoped to find a role serving the poor who worked in Turin's mines.

His sister, Luciana, was one of the brightest spots in Pier Giorgio's life. Together, they weathered the storms of their parents' strict behavioral and academic codes and navigated the tension of life within the household. As they matured, they continued to share camaraderie, even as Pier Giorgio's religious devotion deepened, and Luciana grew more enchanted with the trappings of high society.

When his sister became engaged to a Polish diplomat, Giorgio had difficulty reckoning with his impending separation from her. In this time of conflict in their household, the responsibility of appeasing their parents would fall to him alone. "As every rose has some thorns," he wrote to a friend, "so unfortunately at the joy at seeing my sister happy there is the bitterness of separation because sadly, Italy will never again be her land. Now I will have to fill the void my sister will leave in our home."[2] At her departure, he broke down sobbing at the train station.

What have been the challenges and blessings in your family? How might the Lord be calling you to attend to the relationships in your family with truth and love? Where might you be able to offer more to your family? Boundaries (saying no and respecting your own time and space) are acts of love when done in freedom; how also might you be called to have stronger boundaries in your life with family or others?

Sacrifice

A heartbreaking aspect of Pier Giorgio's story is his offering up of the romantic feelings he had for a good friend in the Catholic community, Laura Hidalgo.

Gentle and passionate in her faith, Laura lost both of her parents young and had to help raise her younger brother while juggling both her studies and work responsibilities. Pier Giorgio and Laura spent much time together volunteering and on mountain excursions. But because she was not part of the upper class, like Frassati's family, and was involved in the Catholic Action group, his family would likely not have approved of Laura as a potential match.

Frassati spoke to Fr. Antonion Cojazzi, his former tutor, about the situation. Here is how their exchange went:

> "Does your mother know how you feel?" the priest asked.
>
> "She doesn't know a thing," Pier Giorgio answered. "She would not be at all pleased, and I know she and father would be strongly opposed."
>
> "So you're telling me that standing between you and this girl is your parents' wishes. Have you thought about ignoring them?" Father Cojazzi asked.
>
> "No! Never. Not under any circumstance," Pier Giorgio responded.
>
> "I feel I should point out that in good conscience you have every right to ignore your parents' opinion, since you're an adult," the priest continued.
>
> "I realize I have that right," Pier Giorgio answered, "but I don't feel I should exercise it."

"Well then," concluded the Salesian priest, "you have no choice but to renounce your feelings for her."

Pier Giorgio lowered his head, a characteristic gesture of agreement, and began to weep.[3]

For the sake of keeping the peace within his family, and recognizing that there was no possible future with Laura that did not involve creating strife and waves for everyone involved, Pier Giorgio never revealed his love for her. By this point, his parents' relationship had devolved into continuous spite and stonewalling; separation seemed imminent. In his goodness and devotion, Pier Giorgio would not allow himself to consider adding fuel to the fire and straining his parents' marriage, asserting that he could not destroy one family to form a new one.

One friend, Isidoro Bonini, did know of Pier Giorgio's burden and secret love, and they exchanged letters in which they shared that grief. Asking for prayer to help carry the burden, he wrote to Isidoro:

> My plan in this is to transform that special liking that I have had for her, which wasn't willed, to the end to which we ought to arrive, in the light of charity, in the respectful bond of friendship understood in the Christian sense, in the respect for her virtue, in the imitation of her illustrious gifts, as I have for the others. Perhaps you might tell me that it's madness to hope this; but I believe, if you pray for me a bit, that in a short time I can achieve this state in prayer. So this is my plan which I hope to achieve with the grace of

God, even if it will cost me the sacrifice of my earthly life, but it matters little."[4]

Today, some might say that Frassati was wrong to repress his romantic feelings for Laura. We could imagine modern voices urging him to "free himself" from the shackles of his family, their expectations, and the toxic home environment. But for Pier Giorgio, to honor his mother and father meant, in the unique situation he was in, to offer up his will in union with the sacrifice of Jesus on the Cross. He saw all things through the eyes of heaven.

The concept of "offering it up"—to choose to endure suffering with purpose or for the sake of another, rather than running from, masochistically indulging in, or denying pain—only makes sense in the light of faith and looking at life with a sacramental vision. When we understand the Christian power to offer up our sufferings in imitation of and union with Jesus, we can make an act of sacrifice that can allow the new life of grace to transform the situation and ourselves. "Suffering that is nourished by the flame of faith becomes something beautiful," Frassati noted, "because it tempers the soul to deal with suffering."

What sacrifices have you been asked to make in your life? What opportunities or relationships have you had to walk away from for a higher good? What internal fruit or bitterness has grown from that sacrifice—and how can you unite yourself more closely to Christ through it?

.   .   .   .

.   .   .   .

.   .   .   .

.   .   .   .

Leap into Action

Return to the first set of reflection questions in this chapter. Reach out to the friend who has made an impact on your life to express your thanks. Text, call, or (even better) write a letter and share some of the details that surfaced in your reflection. Then spend some time thinking of someone in your circle or network who might be in need of friendship. Spend some time praying for this person, then ask God how he might be calling you to respond.

Pray

Lord, you have called us to communion, not isolation. Thank you for the gifts of friendship and family. Help me to be proactive in reaching out with your love to those you place in my life and to be open to the gifts they have to offer. With the intercession of Pier Giorgio Frassati, help me to share the burdens of loved ones, persevere in love through misunderstandings and conflict, and surrender to your love and mercy. Amen!

Last Things

At the age of twenty-four, the robust and athletic Pier Giorgio stumbled down the hallway of his home, deathly sick. He didn't realize it then, but his body was slowly succumbing to paralysis caused by an infection with polio.

His grandmother lay dying in a different room in the same house. For days, Pier Giorgio did his best to try and keep the household's attention on her transition from this life and away from his own suffering. Though he was hardly able to keep any food in his stomach, his fever and ill health went largely unnoticed by family members. His mother even scolded him for daring to be sick during such a stressful time.

During that last week of his life, he dragged himself to visit friends, taking a walking stick with him because he could not stand for long. "He was saying goodbye to everything," wrote his sister Luciana, "leaving the city in which he had been born and which, year after year, he had come to know with all its secrets."[1] Exhausted, he tried to deflect inquiries and keep the attention off of himself. When his friend Bertini called him out for not looking well, Frassati replied, "It's nothing but a case of muscular poisoning. What can we do? We're old!"[2]

Despite his agony, he would drag himself down the corridor nightly to pray by his grandmother's bedside. Three days after the Frassati family would bury their grandmother, they would bury Pier Giorgio.

Luciana writes about how his sickness came as such a surprise:

> He died from an incurable disease; a children's disease destroyed his strong, solid frame. Poliomyelitis is contagious, but strangely, it left those around him untouched. His last days were sheer physical and moral torment, but he was too humble and self-denying to mind the indifference of others. No one took notice of him. Even I, although I had some intuition, was certainly not aware.[3]

It's largely believed that Pier Giogio contracted polio from his work with the poor. The disease can destroy nerve cells in the spinal cord, leading to paralysis, intense pain, and muscle failure (and thus lung failure), which matched his symptoms. Perhaps Pier Giorgio could have been a better steward of his health by seeking more urgent medical attention, but he was just as bewildered by the illness as others. In his humility, he bore this final cross with selflessness.

His right arm was paralyzed near the end, to the point that a visiting religious sister had to help him make the Sign of the Cross. A local priest, Fr. Formica, visited to anoint him with the oil of the sick, affirming, "Giorgio, your soul is beautiful. Jesus wants you with himself. Jesus loves you."[4] His legs grew cold as his lungs succumbed to the paralysis. When he declared that he was worried about what would happen to his parents, the priest assured him, "Giorgio, you will not abandon them; you will live in spirit with them from heaven. You will give them your faith and your self-denial; you will continue to be one family." Frassati nodded and smiled and offered a resigned 'yes.'"[5]

Near the end, Fr. Formica encouraged the weakening young man to take strength by saying, "Courage, Giorgio!" Frassati shut his eyes peacefully to face the great beyond before him.

Pier Giorgio Frassati died at the age of twenty-four with his head held by his mother and his hand intertwined with his sister's, as she clung to his beloved and worn rosary. It was 7 p.m. on July 4, 1925.

What is one area of your life where you are experiencing suffering, discomfort, annoyance? What would it look like to be more selfless in that situation? How can you connect your suffering to that of Jesus, or offer it in solidarity with others who are also suffering in a similar way?

Letting Go

Sometimes suffering is voluntary. Think of Pier Giorgio's willingness to sustain regular fasts or hardships taken on behalf of the poor. Quiet suffering happens everywhere on a daily basis—workers endure overnight shifts to feed their families; single parents juggle multiple jobs to make ends meet.

At times, suffering is a badge of honor, like a Navy Seal enduring Hell Week or an Olympian pouring years of training into one single event. In the Catholic faith, we have a long history of disciples willingly taking on hardships for the sake of penance, offering up difficulties on behalf of others or to seek greater union with the suffering of Jesus Christ.

But often suffering is not voluntary. It is part of the human condition to carry crosses we never opted into. We all will experience various forms of loss, mistakes, and regret. Sometimes we have to navigate the pain and suffering of losing a job or loved one, or experiencing heartbreak, abuse, or rejection.

Alfredo Frassati wanted his son to become the administrative director of his newspaper empire *La Stampa*, but those hoped-for plans would not materialize. Pier Giorgio had hoped to use his long studied-for engineering degree to serve the working miners of both Germany and Italy, but it was not meant to be. He had to negotiate his desires within the context of what was right for his life and family.

It must have caused Pier Giorgio pain and anguish to not be able to follow his desire to directly impact the lives of people living and working in poor conditions. But he had to make a reasoned judgment about what was right. He had to weigh the good desire to serve against the good desire to honor his parents. Discernment always comes down to examining the gifts we've been given and the context of our circumstances to figure out what God is calling us to do. Frassati made a decision to follow his father's wishes and to continue doing as much as he could to assist people living in poverty in other ways. This was a sacrifice. Frassati was handing his life over to God. He had to let go.

The sacrifice of Jesus on the Cross gives us the most powerful image of what it means to voluntarily enter into suffering. The stripes upon his back from the scourging, the lacerating crown of thorns on his head, the nails driven into his feet and hands—Jesus embraced it all willingly for our sake: "No one takes [my life] from me," he said, "but I lay it down of my own accord" (Jn 10:18).

It is not easy to have this level of faith, to be willing, as Frassati stated, to "sacrifice everything for everything: our ambitions, indeed our entire selves, for the cause of the Faith." But our faith reveals that this kind of self-gift in love is the only path to new and abundant life. He went on to declare to a group of young people:

> In order for our life to be Christian, it must be a continued renunciation, a continual sacrifice which however is not burdensome when only we think about what these few years passed in sorrow are, compared with a happy eternity, where joy will have no measure nor end, and where we will enjoy a peace beyond anything we could imagine.[6]

In what part of your life do you most struggle to let go—to hand your preferences over to God? What does the combination of your gifts and the circumstances of your life tell you about what God might be calling you to do in this situation? How can you approach this question with a disposition of sacrificial love?

Let Go and Let God

How we partake in suffering can make all the difference.

We live in a time of abundant material conveniences. These are not bad in and of themselves, but they can lead us to expect comfort at all times and limit our capacity to sustain hardship. In order to expand our ability to fruitfully bear suffering, the Church calls us to regularly take on voluntary fasting and penitential practices. These disciplines help us to willingly embrace discomfort in order to distance ourselves from disordered attachment to pleasures and comforts. These disciplines also teach us to unite our sufferings with the sufferings Christ endured for us.

It's hard to face the discomfort, but when we do, having a posture of surrender can make all the difference in our openness to Christ's presence with us in those moments. We can't control everything, and that's a hard thing to surrender. Letting go—including the release of our pain or anger toward those who have hurt us—is the paradoxical antidote to finding greater peace in our lives.

Fr. Don Dolindo Ruotolo was an Italian priest who served as a spiritual director to Padre Pio (and is on the road to formal sainthood himself). He wrote a novena to encourage prayerful surrender. Fr. Dolindo called himself "Mary's little old man" and suffered for much of his life, even living in paralysis for the last ten years before his death. The recurring refrain of his novena invites us to simply pray, "O Jesus, I surrender myself to you, take care of everything!"[7]

This uncomplicated prayer can help us reframe our lives and release the control we desperately seek. If we trust that God the Father held us in his hand and that all would be well—that he truly is present with us through every moment of our life, even in our sufferings—what freedom might we find?

Sometimes a simple cry of prayer—even as brief as "Come, Holy Spirit" or just making the Sign of the Cross—is all we need to invite God into our lives when we're feeling overwhelmed by a situation or the task before us. Frassati knew how to do this; he entrusted his life to God, and doing so gave him confidence to live boldly. "Jesus is with me," he said. "I have nothing to fear."

Where do you struggle to release control? What burdens weigh on your shoulders? Write as much of the situation down as you can, aiming to articulate why this situation feels like such a burden. Then write a prayer—a simple one, even as short as a phrase—to invite God into this part of your life.

Leap into Action

Frassati's fasting and discipline made him capable of bearing suffering in a way that drew him closer to Christ and deepened his love. What is a habit, pleasure, or good thing you could give up as a way to grow toward more freedom? Write down here your plan for fasting—what you intend to do, and for how long.

Pray

Lord, help me to surrender all that leads me to anxiety and fear, especially the fear of death. Help me to trust in your divine plan, even when I or my loved ones face suffering. With the intercession of Pier Giorgio, please give me the strength to walk boldly into the unknown and uncontrollable circumstances of life, knowing that you are by my side always. Amen!

DAY 7

The Glory

Virtue of the Day: Hope

Two days after Pier Giorgio's death, a large crowd gathered outside of the Frassati home to accompany the body to the parish church for the funeral. Alongside the dignitaries and journalistic associates of Alfredo, a swarm of homeless individuals, factory workers, and ordinary men and women came to pay their respects. The overflowing masses jolted the Frassati family into realizing just how many people's lives were changed by Pier Giorgio.

By nine in the morning, thousands of people flooded the streets. The crowd pressed up to be near his coffin. Some wept and others prayed. A blind man tried to reach the casket in the hopes of a miracle. Young and old, rich and poor alike, intermingled to honor this young man who had given so much.

As eight of Pier Giorgio's classmates carried his casket, Luciana, taking in the spectacle before her, noted, "I could not despair. I felt as if I were walking on air, taking part in a great triumph."[1] The effects of Pier Giorgio's faithful witness rippled throughout his family; even his agnostic father gradually returned to the faith.

The story of this holy young man from Turin who died so suddenly began to spread and even caught the attention of theologians who had crossed paths with him. While the Frassati family lived in Germany, Pier Giorgio became acquainted with the Rahner family, the same household that included Karl and Hugo, two future priests and influential theologians. Karl Rahner joined the Jesuits in 1922 and became renowned for his intellectual prowess. He was one of the most influential thinkers shaping the Second Vatican Council. Rahner's official biographers recalled Frassati's effect on the theologian:

> "[Karl] was profoundly impressed by a young Italian university student, three years his senior, who died in 1925 of acute poliomyelitis in the odor of sanctity: Pier Giorgio Frassati, a . . . fervent daily communicant, apostle in the student world in the struggle against the old sectarian, anticlerical system and against incipient fascism, overflowing with tireless charity toward the poor."[2]

In the introduction he contributed for one of Luciana's books on her brother, Karl Rahner noted that "Frassati represented the pure, happy, handsome Christian youth . . . [the] spirit of rebellion is not found in him. Frassati is a Christian, simply and in an absolutely spontaneous way, as if it were something spontaneous for everybody."[3] Frassati did not live according to the passing currents and fads of the time. Rahner saw in him the joyful abandonment of a bold disciple whose passion burned from a divine wellspring.

Imagine your own funeral. Write down what you hope you're remembered for by the people who gather to pray for you.

The Only Legacy That Matters

Funerals are eye-opening experiences. Death shakes us awake. While we're tempted to postpone or distract ourselves from thinking about death, the reality is that our time is limited. We don't know the length of our days on Earth. The Latin phrase *memento mori* has long been used by Christians to harken our attention toward the end of our lives, to "remember our death" so that we might order our days well.

How do *you* want to be remembered? We often spend so much time chasing success, popularity, pleasure, or comfort, but there's only one legacy that truly matters. As the Catholic novelist Leon Bloy wrote, "The only real sadness, the only real failure, the only great tragedy in life, is not to become a saint."

Holiness is a life that is whole, integrated, and full of peace. When we let our desires run rampant, we become scattered and unhappy. The saint who is fully alive lives with all of the right cylinders firing. That's not a stuffy or dull existence, nor is it an easy one—*many* of the saints suffered greatly—but it is one full of purpose and joy.

Think back to where we began this journey with the question: What do you imagine when you hear the word "saint"? Is holiness something unattainable or unreachable? Perhaps holiness is simply the deepest call of the Lord on your life. It's not a mandate to have your life look exactly like Mother Teresa or Pier Giorgio, but it's the call to live the Gospel in the here and now, wherever you find yourself. By responding to that call in ways however big or small, we become more fully the people we were created to be.

There are no doubt many holy men and women who have walked the earth that the Church will never formally recognize as saints. Numerous unnamed martyrs, for instance, gave their lives for the faith under persecutions from the Roman Empire or to the Communist regime of the twentieth century. They are lost to history, but not to the mind of God. Holiness also appears in more ordinary, familiar ways. We see it among our family, friends, or community, those who consistently and humbly witness to the Lord's love.

In an age where we are quick to tear down our heroes, I believe that the Lord continues to raise up young saints among us for a reason. He knows we need these encouraging and relatable figures to inspire us. The people of Turin responded to the holiness they saw in Pier Giorgio—his witness changed their lives.

A maid who worked in the Frassati home faced a personal crisis, but was inspired by Pier Giorgio to cling to faith. He told her, "The life of the good is the most difficult, but it is the quickest way to get to heaven."[4]

If you were to die tomorrow, what are the things that you would regret not doing with your life? If you knew that you had one year to live, what would you change about your life? What if you had ten years to live—what would your priorities be?

The Miracles

In 1938, thirteen years after Pier Giorgio's death, a Vatican decree began the process of exploring his life for possible canonization.

Sometimes the Church canonizes a person quickly, but it usually takes many years, sometimes hundreds. For Pier Giorgio, the process would take decades of procedures, interviews, and inquiries to formally declare what so many of his contemporaries already knew.

Pier Giorgio's remains were exhumed in 1981 as part of the inspection process, and they would eventually to be transferred from the family tomb in Pollone to the Cathedral of St. John the Baptist in Turin in 1990. His body was found completely incorrupt. His skin remained soft and rosy, as if he were asleep, fifty-six years after the day he died.

This phenomenon, which has been documented in numerous other saints like Catherine of Siena and Vincent de Paul, is a miraculous event where the decaying process does not take hold of the holy person's remains. Sometimes the whole body is incorrupt, and in some instances it's only a portion of the body. In some cases, an incorrupt body even emits beautiful smells or a pure oil like chrism. God permits these extraordinary events for the sake of our faith, for they encourage our belief in the goodness of the human body and our hope for the life to come.

When the people of God raise up the witness of a holy man or woman for consideration as a saint, the Church begins a formal investigation into their life—examining correspondences, witness testimonies, and other evidence. One of the most important qualifiers for a person to become a saint is the documentation of two miracles attributed to their intercession. There is a formal process to study such miraculous events—usually in the form of surprising medical healings—to prove that there is no other possible scientific explanation at play. (Believe it or not, an incorrupt body doesn't count as a qualifying miracle!) Miracles reveal to us that a potential saint is indeed alive in Christ and interceding for us from heaven because we can see the effect of their prayers on our behalf.

While many miracles have already been informally attributed to the intercession of Pier Giorgio, the first extraordinary event officially recognized by the Church to count toward his cause for canonization came by way of a man named Domenico Sellan. In 1933, Domenico was forty years old and suffering from paralysis and a tubercular disease of the spine. A friend of his, who was a priest, brought a prayer card of Frassati and placed it near Domenico as he prayed for his healing. Domenico was cured and lived for thirty-five more years. In 1989, the documentation of the miracle received approval.[5]

The second official miracle involved a priest from Los Angeles, Fr. Juan Manual Gutierrez, who suffered a painful Achilles tendon injury as a seminarian in 2017. Knowing he would need surgery, he decided to pray a novena to Frassati, asking for his intercession. "My prayer was, 'Lord, through the intercession of Blessed Pier Giorgio Frassati, I ask you to help me in my injury,'" he explained. Then he added a spontaneous addition to his prayer, declaring, "And I promise that, if anything unusual happens, I will report it to whomever I need to report it to."

"That part did surprise me," recalled Gutierrez. "I'm like, where did that come from?"[6]

A few days later, Gutierrez was praying in the chapel and noticed a warm sensation enveloping his foot. "It was gentle," he said. "But it would increase little by little, and at some point I thought that an outlet of the electrical was catching fire. And I was looking for the fire. And there was no fire there. So I just remember looking at my ankle and thinking, 'That's so strange' because I could feel the warmth."[7]

Days later, when the surgeon examined Gutierrez's foot, he found no problem with the tendon; it had completely healed. "You had a tear in your Achilles," the surgeon said, "but now I can't find it."

After some time, Gutierrez wrote his testimony down and shared it with a priest who had connections with the Dicastery for the Causes of the Saints. Over the next few years, Vatican officials gathered documents and MRIs and interviewed witnesses. On November 20, 2024, Pope Francis announced—to the surprise and joy of many—the approval of Frassati's cause for canonization, a few days later verifying that it was indeed Gutierrez's healing that provided the second miracle many were waiting for.

Look back over the last year of your life. Make a list of the ways you've experienced God acting in your life—from the people and experiences that have come your way, to significant moments of growth, to moving experiences of truth, beauty, or goodness. If you've had supernatural or extraordinary experiences of God's nearness, great! But don't overlook the more ordinary ways God has been active in your life.

Leap into Action

Take a moment to ponder the life of someone you know who has died. How did their life form and shape you? What part of their example do you hope to carry with you into the future? Gather your thoughts, then reach out to someone close to the deceased. Send a text, write a letter, make a call, stop by for a visit, and share with them the impact this person had on your life.

Pray

Loving Father, thank you for rescuing us from the final pain of death through your Son, Jesus Christ. Because you have overcome this final enemy, we await the resurrection of our bodies and the life to come. Thank you for giving us the examples of the saints to remind us of your glorious power, and we ask, with the intercession of Pier Giorgio, for an increase of trust in you and the hope of your Second Coming. Amen!

DAY 8
At the Summit

Virtue of the Day: Freedom

Throughout this eight-day journey, we've examined the challenge of ascending beyond mediocrity ("the middle of the mountain"). Pier Giorgio Frassati has been our trusted guide. We've seen how his fidelity to Christ led to overflowing love, generosity, and patience that he shared with all he met and how he surrendered to a life of service to the point of laying down his life.

Here at the summit of our ascent, we have the opportunity to take in the panoramic view from the past seven days. Let's look back over the climb thus far to see the terrain we've covered. What insights and practices do you want to continue to carry with you? In what specific ways do you feel inspired by Frassati's example and feel called to take action in your own life?

- On the first day, we assessed our starting assumptions about what it means to be a saint and how all of us are called to a life of holiness aimed at union with Christ.

- On day two, we contemplated Frassati's love of nature and the importance of reclaiming wonder and curiosity.

- Day three brought us to examine our conceptions of God and how we are nourished by the Eucharist and the inspirational witness of the saints.

- On day four we pondered Frassati's love for the poor and those on the margins of society, and we contemplated where we might be called to serve locally.

- Day five led us through the theme of family and devotion to our loved ones, with all the joys and sufferings that can come in those relationships.

- Day six brought us face-to-face with Frassati's suffering and death and how we too must reconcile with the inevitable shortness of life by surrendering what is beyond our control.

- Day seven reoriented us to hope in the life of Christ, who defeated death itself, and to celebrate Frassati's victorious presence in heaven, where he intercedes on our behalf!

We are *all* called to be saints. The Church boldly proclaims the "universal call to the holiness," which is the understanding that Christ calls everyone to a life of union with him: "All Christians in any state or walk of life are called to the fullness of Christian life and to the perfection of charity. All are called to holiness" (*CCC*, 2013).

The ways that holiness takes shape and the circumstances in which we will live our sanctity out will be as varied as each one of us. We see this diversity in holiness reflected in the saints themselves—from Francis of Assisi, to Charles Lwanga, to Joan of Arc, to Martin de Porres, to Kateri Tekakwitha, to

Carlo Acutis, every Christian's journey with God is unique according to their own time and place.

We cannot find holiness in isolation. Recall the insight from day three that we are made in the image and likeness of the Trinitarian God, who is a communion of persons. We are fundamentally built for community, so our path to holiness necessarily puts us in relationship with others. Rubbing up against other people's needs, wants, quirks, demands, and irritations challenges us to grow. We can only learn selflessness by giving ourselves away to others. And we need the example and encouragement we get from one another on this journey toward holiness.

It's been said that the best scripture scholars are the saints (even the ones who failed Latin) because they put into action the Word of God. They did what Christ said to do, without rationalizing, intellectualizing away, or making excuses. We need theologians, evangelists, and academics, of course, but even more urgently do we need holy men and women who embody God's love in the world; we need those who are *doers* of the word and not hearers only (Jas 1:22). Think also of the Belgian priest St. Damien who voluntarily went to live and minister to the lepers on a colony on the Hawaiian island of Molokai. Or consider the more contemporary witness of St. Teresa of Calcutta, who dedicated decades of her life to serving the poorest of the poor in India.

And of course, we have the example and inspiration of Pier Giorgio Frassati, a young man living with great means in a time of political upheaval, who still made time for consistent prayer and lived generously toward all he encountered, without desiring any acclaim for himself. When he spent time in

Germany, he was moved toward the plight of the poor living in nearby Austria, and he wrote to his friend, Maria Fischer, "There are many children and women workers in Vienna today without a roof over their heads, left prey to hunger and misery. I'm sending you 90,000 crowns that I had left over from my trip and I ask you to use the money as you wish. In this my name should remain secret."[1]

Our own work might be substantially more hidden than Frassati's, and our legacies might not be as grand as these major heroes of the Church, but we all have a part to play in the Body of Christ and in the ongoing story of salvation history. There are souls that will not be reached unless we do our part, just as those who handed on the faith to us through words and deeds gave us the pearl of great price (Mt 13:45–46).

Review your reflections from the previous days of this journey. Make note here of the insights and experiences that were most meaningful and impactful for you in your effort to bring holiness into your everyday life. Then prioritize the practices you want to continue to carry with you into the future.

What's Holding You Back?

Holiness is really a life of wholeness, a life of integration. We have our own work to do, but the primary agent of our formation is the Trinitarian God. That is good news for us! Through prayer, reflection, and the sacraments, God's healing love brings together what sin fractures. God's grace builds upon our nature. As we develop and grow in virtue, we make more room in our lives for God to transform us. As these habits of excellence take root and God's life sprouts within us, choosing and willing the good becomes easier, bit by bit.

Of course there are setbacks and failures. We all experience moments when we fall to lust, anger, envy, or self-centeredness. But God allows even these humbling moments to be instructional as well. For when we sin or fall short, we remember that we can't make it to heaven on our own—we need to ask for his help. The saints are not men and women who never fell—they are the men and women who knew where to look for the grace to help them get back up.

Pursuing a life of holiness is a great challenge; it is the work and adventure of a lifetime. It requires continual conversion and change to venture ever deeper into the mystery of God's love. *Change is hard,* and at every corner we face the temptation to give up. It is far easier to turn toward mindless entertainment or doomscrolling, as perfectly curated distractions are a finger touch away. It takes discipline and consistent courage to put one foot in front of the other to better ourselves through prayer and meaningful action.

Sometimes it's the very ordinariness of life that wears us down. Routines are necessary for our mental structure, but they can certainly feel stale if we simply run through life on autopilot. Get up, go to school or work, do chores, eat and exercise—lather, rinse, and repeat. Our routines can even shackle us, creating a sort of "prison of comfort" that keeps us from change. Being anchored in a routine can mask a fear of failure when we cling to it because we're worried that our attempts at change or finding a new way to live will fall flat.

We all have self-centered tendencies. We prefer getting our way; our egos are stubborn, and a lifetime of habits or addictions do not go down quietly. Surrender is painful! Our digital culture gives us instant access to gratification of nearly any kind, which atrophies our capacity for patience and discomfort. But real, sustained growth doesn't happen overnight—it takes consistent, incremental effort in areas of our lives that are hidden.

If we feel the lure of escaping it all, if we've become accustomed to dysfunctional relationships or the high drama that reality TV trains us to expect, then the simple work of faithfulness can seem dull to the point that we can sabotage ourselves for the sake of some fleeting excitement. Or perhaps we passively wait for God to wave a magic wand to instantly grant our wishes. It's easy to grow increasingly frustrated by the fact that change happens on his timeline, not our own.

It's easy to look over Frassati's life now and see it as a complete whole, an unswerving path toward goodness. But when he was living it, the way forward was not clear. He struggled with doubt and uncertainty about the choices he was making and the call he was hearing from God. He kept climbing and searching, rooting himself in the prayer and practices that anchored his life in faith. But it wasn't easy, as we read in one

of his letters to a good friend that reveals him wrestling with
the challenge of seeking holiness in the everyday:

> I need prayers because I am going through a criti-
> cal moment in my life—you understand me, I am on
> the verge of concluding my student life, which is nice
> [and] without worries, in order to begin a hard climb
> in life, a much harder road, especially since something
> has changed in me, something that anticipates a very
> sudden storm. . . . I will face the difficulties, I hope,
> by turning to prayers and in the hope that one day or
> another I will pass to a better life. . . . I ask you to pray
> a lot for me so that every day I can solidify my faith
> and have the strength to bear the difficulties that in
> these latest years of my youth have been impeding
> my path.[2]

*What are the biggest challenges you've faced in this journey toward
holiness with Frassati? What are the distractions, fears, or routines that appear as your biggest obstacles? How can you navigate
through them? Who are the friends you can count on for support and
prayers, and how can you involve them in your ascent?*

Freedom to Do What Is Right

Frassati's feast day falls on July 4, the date of his death. For Americans, this is a date that is synonymous with liberty because it is when we celebrate Independence Day. But Pier Giorgio's life offers us a different perspective on freedom; he is an example of a man par excellence who used his freedom rightly and generously.

Our culture thinks of freedom as the ability to do whatever we want, whenever we want to do it. It's not wrong in and of itself, but this understanding of freedom is too narrow and self-centered—it's all about "me." This kind of freedom is self-referential and lacks direction and purpose beyond the fulfillment of our basest desires.

Freedom becomes *life-giving* when it is oriented toward love. "Freedom consists not in doing what we like," St. John Paul II declared in a 1995 address during his visit to America, "but in having the right to do what we ought."[3] Proper freedom asks, *In what ways can I get over myself and serve others? What holds me back from participating in God's love and becoming the person I was created to be?*

Even if we find ourselves sick-bound like Frassati, persecuted or exiled like St. John Chrysostom, or shackled in prison like St. Paul, we are still *free*. No matter our circumstances, we still have free will and a chance to make of our lives what we will. We decide how to direct our beliefs, words, and actions; we have the power to shift our attitude and perspectives—to see with the eyes of gratitude and to make a gift of ourselves, even in our poverty. And we have an abundance of heroic examples from the past century to show us that choosing such heroic love, even in the face of great evil, is the real freedom for which Christ has set us free (Gal 5:1).

Cardinal Francis Xavier Nguyen Van Thuan was imprisoned by Communist forces in Vietnam for thirteen years, including nine in solitary confinement. He recited the Mass from memory on the palm of his hand inside his cell, with crumbs of bread and a drop of smuggled-in wine from a sympathetic prison guard. Years later, once he was set free, Cardinal Van Thuan asserted that "only Christian love can change hearts, not weapons and not threats. . . . It is love that prepares the way for the announcement of the gospel. *Omnia vincit amor*: Love conquers everything."[4]

Fr. Walter Ciszek spent twenty-three years in Soviet prisons and gulags, falsely accused of being a Vatican spy. He experienced loneliness, doubt, frustration, and despair. This experience broke his spirits but gave him profound wisdom through humility. "I had tried to do too much on my own and I had failed. . . . I had never really abandoned myself to [God's providence]. . . . Perfection consisted simply in learning to discover God's will in every situation and then in bending every effort to do what must be done."[5]

Instead of seeking God's will for his life as a plan he had to discover outside of himself and set out to follow, he learned to find God's presence *where he was*—even trapped in a Soviet prison. He wrote, "Accepting whatever comes or happens as the will of God, no matter what it costs spiritually, psychologically, or physically, is the surest and quickest way to freedom of soul and spirit that surpasses all understanding and explanation."[6]

Frassati had every right to curse the poor who made him sick, or rail at God for rewarding his faithfulness with suffering. By the world's standards, he ought to have used his freedom to satisfy his desires and create a comfortable life for himself. Instead, he continually gave away whatever time, energy, and resources he had to elevate the lives of others. Even in his last days, racked with pain and becoming increasingly paralyzed, he gave away his possessions to people in need and limped home to be near his grandmother during *her* suffering.

Pier Giorgio used the means available to him to serve those around him. He didn't lament his circumstances or succumb to passivity. He did not rely on excuses or fall into self-pity. He used his creativity in every way to give just a little bit more of himself—to God first, and then to others. He used his freedom for self-gift, and doing so gave him purpose and meaning and joy. Here's how he put it to a friend:

> Every day I understand better what a grace it is to be Catholics. Poor unlucky those who don't have a faith: to live without a faith, without a patrimony to defend, without a steady struggle for the truth, is not living but existing. We must never exist but live, because even through every disappointment we should remember that . . . we have a faith to sustain, a hope to attain: our Homeland. And therefore let us banish all melancholy which can only exist when the faith is lost. Human sorrows touch us, but if they are viewed in the light of religion, and thus of self-surrender, they are not harmful but helpful, because they purify the soul.[7]

We are free insofar as we give ourselves away, "for whoever would save his life will lose it, and whoever loses his life for my sake will find it" (Mt 16:25). How have you made a gift of yourself to God and to others over the course of this journey with Pier Giorgio? What fruit has this process born in your life? What does this experience tell you about the direction of your life?

.   .   .   .

.   .   .   .

.   .   .   .

.   .   .   .

Leap into Action

Who is one person in your life who could benefit from the example of Pier Giorgio Frassati? Pray for them and consider introducing them to his life and witness.

Pray

Lord, thank you for creating us and bringing us into existence. Thank you for the glory of your creation and for calling us to know you in an intimate relationship. May I cheerfully radiate this love to others. Thank you for the witnesses of the holy men and women throughout your Church's history, especially for the example of Pier Giorgio Frassati. May his prayers join with mine as I offer you the fruit of these eight days in prayer. Amen!

CONCLUSION
Set Out on the Climb

In 1925, shortly after Pier Giorgio passed from this life, Baldovino di Rovasenda, the president of the Catholic university club for men in Turin, wrote, "It would be an outrage to the memory of Pier Giorgio to be enthusiastic about him without attempting to model ourselves on his example."[1]

I would like to think that Frassati himself would shy away from such praise and would point rather toward the example of Christ, who was the source and summit of all his strength. But the point remains that we can't merely put these heroes of the faith on a pedestal and assume that because they worked so hard, we don't need to—or that it is unrealistic to ever live up to their example.

St. John Paul II named Frassati as "a young man who was able to witness to Christ with singular effectiveness in this century of ours. When I was a young man, I, too, felt the beneficial influence of his example and, as a student, I was impressed by the force of his testimony."[2] The life of this young man, now a century past his final hour on the earth, sent ripples through the Church, inspiring future popes and everyday young people.

There is a reason why Frassati has inspired young men and women the world over, becoming the patron of so many young-adult groups and fellowship organizations. His robust joy and delight in his faith, as well as the endurance through suffering to the end of his brief life, moves many (including myself) to want to be better. Achieving sainthood is not difficult—remember, all of us are called to holiness—we just have to *set out on the climb*. Make the time, commit to our life source of daily prayer, and let God's grace do the rest.

From his heavenly vantage now, Pier Giorgio continues to intercede for all of us who dare to test our desire for greatness and seek the face of God.

Be not afraid to take action in your life after the example of Pier Giorgio Frassati and entrust the results to Christ.

St. Pier Giorgio Frassati, pray for us!

Acknowledgments

Thank you to my editor Josh Noem and the amazing team at Ave Maria Press for entrusting me with this project.

Thank you to Luciana Frassati Gawronska (1902–2007), Christine Wohar, and all who have documented the writings and example of Pier Giorgio so that we, and the generations to come, may be blessed with knowing Frassati's life in such a vivid way.

Thank you to all my former students and the young (and not-so-young) people whom I have been privileged to accompany, mentor, and hike off the beaten path with in this life.

Thank you to my parents who have always fostered in me the gift of writing, encouraged me to stick to the craft, and allowed me to travel to some wild mountains around the world.

Thank you to my wife Jackie and our children for allowing me yet again to spend much time away at the computer to work on this manuscript. I love you all.

And thank you to Pier Giorgio Frassati, whose gentle hand and intercession I have felt assist me on this project since the beginning. May many souls be brought to Christ through his radical "yes" to living the Gospel.

Notes

Day 1: Fully Alive

1. Bishop Thomas J. Olmsted, *Manual for Men* (TAN Books, 2017), 179.

2. Pope Benedict XVI, "Message of His Holiness Pope Benedict VXI for the Twenty-Sixth World Youth Day (2011)," The Holy See, August 6, 2010, https://www.vatican.va/content/benedict-xvi/en/messages/youth/documents/hf_ben-xvi_mes_20100806_youth.html.

3. Pope John Paul II, "15th World Youth Day Address of the Holy Father John Paul II Vigil of Prayer," The Holy See, August 19, 2000, https://www.vatican.va/content/john-paul-ii/en/speeches/2000/jul-sep/documents/hf_jp-ii_spe_20000819_gmg-veglia.html.

4. St. Bernard of Clairvaux, "Sermon," in *The Office of Readings According to the Roman Rite*, trans. The International Commission on English in the Liturgy (Boston: Daughters of St. Paul, 1983), 1614–15.

5. J. Michael Strachan, "The Feast of St. Polycarp (February 23)," The Archives Near Emmaus, February 23, 2013, https://nearemmaus.wordpress.com/2013/02/23/the-feast-of-st-polycarp-february-23rd/.

Day 2: The Mountains Are Calling

1. Pier Giorgio Frassati, *Letters to His Friends and Family*, trans. Fr. Timothy E. Deeter (Alba House, 2009), xv.

2. "A Saint on Skis," FrassatiUSA, 2023, https://frassatiusa.org/about-blessed-pier-giorgio-frassati.

3. Frassati, *Letters*, 132.

4. Brooke Hess, "Flow State: The Reason Why Alex Honnold and Steph Davis Are Not Adrenaline Junkies," The Outdoor Journal, February 15, 2019, https://www.outdoorjournal.com/flow-state-reason-alex-honnold-steph-davis-not-adrenaline-junkies/#:~:text=An%20

athlete%20addicted%20to%20Flow,for%20the%20feeling%20of%20
effortlessness.

5. Pope John Paul II, "Angelus," The Holy See, July 11, 1999,
https://www.vatican.va/content/john-paul-ii/en/angelus/1999/docu-
ments/hf_jp-ii_ang_19990711.html.

6. Peter Kreeft, *I Surf Therefore I Am: A Philosophy of Surfing* (St.
Augustine's Press, 2008), 45.

7. Frassati, *Letters*, 134.

8. Luciana Frassati, *A Man of the Beatitudes: Pier Giorgio Frassati*
(Ignatius Press, 2001), 133.

9. Frassati, *Letters*, 132.

10. Augustine, *Confessions*, trans. Henry Chadwick (Oxford University Press, 2008), 187.

11. Pope John Paul II, "Angelus," The Holy See, July 15, 2001,
https://www.vatican.va/content/john-paul-ii/en/angelus/2001/docu-
ments/hf_jp-ii_ang_20010715.html.

Day 3: The Host of Heaven

1. "His Eucharistic Devotion," FrassatiUSA, 2025, https://fras-
satiusa.org/his-eucharistic-devotion

2. Christine M. Wohar, *Finding Frassati: And Following His Path
to Holiness* (EWTN Publishing Inc., 2021), 134.

3. Maria Di Lorenzo, *Blessed Pier Giorgio Frassati: An Ordinary
Christian*, trans. Robert Ventresca (Pauline Books & Media, 2004), 53.

4. Fr. Pasquale Di Girolamo, SJ, *Blessed Pier Giorgio Frassati: From
Prayer to the Apostolate* (New Hope Publications, 1996), 20.

5. "His Marian Devotion," FrassatiUSA, 2025, https://frassatiusa.
org/his-marian-devotion.

6. Di Lorenzo, *Blessed Pier Giorgio Frassati*, 55.

7. Frassati, *Letters*, 198.

8. Frassati, *Letters*, 196.

9. Frassati, *Letters*, 129.

Day 4: The Cheerful Giver

1. Frassati, *Letters*, 241.

2. Di Lorenzo, *Blessed Pier Giorgio Frassati*, 31.

3. Frassati, *Man of the Beatitudes*, 144–45.

4. Pope Francis, "Message of His Holiness Pope Francis for the Fifth World Day of the Poor," The Holy See, November 14, 2021, https://www.vatican.va/content/francesco/en/messages/poveri/documents/20210613-messaggio-v-giornatamondiale-poveri-2021.html.

5. Di Lorenzo, *Blessed Pier Giorgio Frassati*, 40–41.

6. Di Lorenzo, *Blessed Pier Giorgio Frassati*, 47.

7. Di Lorenzo, *Blessed Pier Giorgio Frassati*, 41.

8. Mother Teresa, *A Simple Path* (Ballantine Books, 1995), 79.

Day 5: Fraternity and Family

1. Di Lorenzo, *Blessed Pier Giorgio Frassati*, 30.

2. Frassati, *Letters*, 187.

3. Di Lorenzo, *Blessed Pier Giorgio Frassati*, 88.

4. Frassati, *Letters*, 216.

Day 6: Last Things

1. Luciana Frassati, *My Brother Pier Giorgio: His Last Days*, trans. Fr. Hector R. G. Pérez (New Hope Publications, 2002), 22.

2. Frassati, *My Brother Pier Giorgio*, 25.

3. Frassati, *Man of the Beatitudes*, 155.

4. Frassati, *My Brother Pier Giorgio*, 105.

5. Frassati, *My Brother Pier Giorgio*, 98.

6. Frassati, *Letters,* 130.

7. Cate Von Dohlen, "How to Pray the Surrender Novena," Hallow, 2025, https://hallow.com/blog/how-to-pray-the-surrender-novena/.

Day 7: The Glory

1. Luciana Frassati, *Una vita mai spenta: Ultimi sei giorni di Pier Giorgio*, Special Edition for "La Stampa" (RCS Libri, 1992), 115.

2. Frassati, *Man of the Beatitudes*, 19.

3. Frassati, *Man of the Beatitudes*, 15–16.

4. Frassati, *Man of the Beatitudes*, 147.

5. "What Was the First Miracle Attributed to Blessed Frassati's Intercession?" FrassatiUSA, 2025, https://frassatiusa.org/first-miracle.

6. Pablo Kay, "The Untold LA Story of the Miracle That Will Make Pier Giorgio Frassati a Saint," Angelus News, December 15, 2024, https://angelusnews.com/local/la-catholics/frassati-la-miracle/.

7. Kay, "Untold LA Story."

Day 8: At the Summit

1. Frassati, *Letters*, 116.

2. Frassati, *Letters*, 161.

3. Pope John Paul II, "Homily of His Holiness John Paul II: Oriole Park at Camden Yards, Baltimore," The Holy See, October 8, 1995, https://www.vatican.va/content/john-paul-ii/en/homilies/1995/documents/hf_jp-ii_hom_19951008_baltimore.html.

4. "Canonization Cause of Cardinal Nguyen Van Thuan Moves Forward," Salt + Light Media, May 4, 2017, https://slmedia.org/blog/cardinal-van-thuan-canonization-cause.

5. Walter J. Ciszek, *He Leadeth Me* (Image Books, 2014), 71, 81.

6. Ciszek, *He Leadeth Me*, 166.

7. Frassati, *Letters*, 214.

Conclusion

1. Wohar, *Finding Frassati*, xiii.

2. Solène Tadié, "Blessed Pier Giorgio Frassati Is First Modern Lay Saint, According to Niece," *National Catholic Register*, July 4, 2019, https://www.ncregister.com/interview/blessed-pier-giorgio-frassati-is-first-modern-lay-saint-according-to-niece.

Bobby Angel is a Catholic author, speaker, and certified mentor for the CatholicPsych Institute with more than twenty years of experience in ministry. He is the author of *Gaming and the Heroic Life* and coauthor of *Pray, Decide, and Don't Worry: Five Steps to Discerning God's Will* (with his wife, Jackie, and Fr. Mike Schmitz) and *Forever: A Catholic Devotional for Your Marriage* (with Jackie). Angel also contributed to the books *Catholicism after Coronavirus*, *Wisdom and Wonder*, and *The New Apologetics*.

He earned bachelor's degrees from the University of Florida and St. John Vianney College Seminary and master's degrees from the St. Vincent de Paul Regional Seminary and the Augustine Institute. He trained at the Theology of the Body Institute. He also has worked as a certified firefighter and emergency medical technician.

Angel has spoken at the National Catholic Youth Conference, the Good News Conference, Life Teen retreats, and diocesan youth conferences. He was a regular on Jonathon "Bearded" Blevins's *Around the Halo* on Twitch, the Ascension Presents YouTube channel, and the Word on Fire *God and Gaming* video series with Fr. Blake Britton. He contributes to the *National Catholic Register* and serves as a guide for the JP2 Trails retreats.

He lives with his family in the Dallas, Texas, area.

Website: Jackieandbobby.com

Instagram: @bobby.angel

YouTube: @jackieandbobby

ALSO BY
BOBBY ANGEL

Gaming and the Heroic Life
A Quest for Holiness in the Virtual World

Video games fuel a fundamental human drive for adventure—like the epic quest to slay zombies, a solo voyage to rescue the princess, or setting off with a clan to defeat the final boss.

The desire to be a hero in your journey is something Bobby Angel can relate to. A lifelong gamer, he was the cohost of the *God and Gaming* series on YouTube and often appears as a guest on Bearded Blevins's *Around the Halo* on Twitch. In *Gaming and the Heroic Life*, Bobby explains that you don't have to just play the role of hero in a game—you can actually pursue a heroic life by the way you engage the virtual world.

Gaming and the Heroic Life is a map to becoming not only a better gamer but also a better person—one who has a purpose and knows where they fit into the world.

The book contains three levels:

- **LEVEL ONE** explores why people love games and what games have to do with God.
- **LEVEL TWO** examines how the Easter eggs of truth, beauty, and goodness in games impact players in much the same way that they impact your relationship with God.
- **LEVEL THREE** demonstrates how gaming can propel players AFK (away from keyboard) to find purpose and meaning in serving others.

Bobby shows where video games intersect with a life of faith in God, revealing how games echo our call to holiness and how we can respond to that call in both the virtual and real worlds.